Ici Lu

SURVIVING ORGANIZATIONAL INSANITY

KEEPING *Spirit Alive* AT WORK

Dear Ici,
a fellow teacher!
Hang in there.
Sharon Rolbin

SHARON
ROLBIN
Ph.D.

Lightkeeper
Ottawa

Surviving Organizational Insanity: Keeping Spirit Alive at Work

Printed and bound in Canada

Lightkeeper
2445 Ogilvie Road,
Gloucester, Ontario, K1J 7N3
Canada

Canadian Cataloguing in Publication Data

Rolbin, Sharon, 1948-
Surviving organizational insanity : keeping spirit alive at work

ISBN 0-9680347-0-5

1. Employee morale. 2. Employee motivation.
3. Organizational behavior. 4. Psychology, Industrial.
I. Title

HD31.R64 1996 158.7 C96-900015-4

THE PRODUCTION TEAM
Cover Design: Leo Yerxa
Photo: Cynthia E. Rolbin
Editing: June Rogers
Desktop Publishing and Printing: Publishing Plus

DEDICATION

This book is dedicated to the memory of David, my last cancer patient, to his wife, Libby, and to their four children. David's story changed the course of my life and sowed the seed of this book. May its publication add to his legacy.

ACKNOWLEDGMENTS

I am grateful to the 20 people who so generously shared their organizational trials and tribulations and provided the stories on which this book is based. Many of their names have been changed and some stories are composites in order to safeguard their privacy.

Thanks also to Greg Richards, who encouraged me daily at work and got me to get serious and turn the dream into reality by setting a writing schedule; to Janet Leduc, Susan Stern, Isabelle Leclerc and Ursula Livingston for extremely valuable input on various drafts; to Reva Nelson, author, speaker and friend for advice and recommendations; and to Gerry Tessier who got my spirit soaring again.

Special thanks to family and friends who supported and encouraged me through the times when I wondered whether this book would ever see the light of day, and especially to three wise young women, Cynthia, Stefanie and Alison Rolbin, my daughters, who are more than any mother could ask for. Without their love, patience, support, encouragement and partnership in creating a co-operative household, this project would never have been completed. Last, but certainly not least, grace and gratitude to Wally Brant, my loving life partner. As Julie Andrews sings to Christopher Plummer in the movie version of Rodgers and Hammerstein's *The Sound of Music,* "I must have done something good."

TABLE OF CONTENTS

Introduction **1**

In The Beginning **7**

Engaged Spirit 7

The People 11

The Passion 13

What Turns The Spirit Off? **17**

Deleterious Direction 18

Rigid Rules 23

Bothered Bosses 27

Survival Strategies **33**

Fighters 38

Perception Changers 42

Zombies 47

Ten Tips For Managers **51**

Why Haven't We Got It Yet? **69**

Pace Of Change 70

A Wiser Workforce 70

Management Musings and Canine Counsel 72

The Farm Or The Olympics 84

INTRODUCTION

The seed of this book was sown in 1987, the day I met my last cancer patient. There stood David, a former corporate vice-president, 46 years old, six feet tall, weighing less than 150 pounds, his stomach swollen with cancer the size of a full-term pregnancy. "Doc," he said, getting comfortable on the foot stool since he could no longer sit on a chair, "I want you to teach me to use my mind and spirit to heal my body." I was overwhelmed. David needed more than a psychotherapist. He needed a miracle.

At that point in my career, I had had a flourishing private counselling and consulting practice for eight years, working primarily with people battling cancer. My clients and I looked at what was going on in their lives the year before their illness was first diagnosed. We looked at the possible connections between stress and illness. Using relaxation and visual imagery combined with other psychotherapy and counselling techniques, we worked on managing the stress in their lives and strengthening their will to live. This was done in conjunction with the medical therapy they were receiving. In addition, I taught courses and led groups at the Ontario Cancer Institute in Toronto.

Much has been written and more research is currently under way on both the connection between stress and illness and the degree to which this kind of therapy can actually prolong life. We worked on improving the quality of life that each individual had left. Some of my patients lived longer than their doctors had predicted, but many, like David came to me very late in their illness. My work with David revolved mostly around teaching him visualization techniques to help ease his pain. He died a few short months after we met, about two weeks after our last visit.

David had spent the two previous years of his life in a work situation that he experienced as highly stressful. He had a great deal of responsibility, yet no authority to meet this responsibility adequately. As his company neared bankruptcy, he believed he had the answers, but he could not convince the appropriate people to listen. His hands were tied, yet he was too loyal to leave. He felt the stress literally "eat him up inside."

Perhaps David would have gotten cancer anyway, with or without the corporate stress. Who knows? But for me, his and his family's anguish were enough. I could no longer stay on the sidelines, waiting for people to come to me when it was too late. David was my last private client. I vowed to get inside organizations, to work with managers and employees alike, doing my best to nip organizational stressors in the bud, finding out more about how the human spirit gets dampened, and when I was ready, to write about it.

Eighteen months later, after some contract work with different private and public sector organizations, I began providing psychological services to a large public sector organization in Toronto, and soon after, became head of the Employee Assistance Program for this same organization. I provided professional advice and direction to a network of psychologists and social workers across the country. Professionally, all sailed merrily along for the first couple of years, with the promotion mid-way through the first year. Then, things began to go steadily downhill. I had become convinced I was losing my touch when a very dear colleague pulled me aside one day and said, "Sharon, don't you see what has been happening to you? You are a shadow of your former self. Your spirit is gone!" I was becoming one of the organizational casualties I had come to write about. Although I did not have cancer, I was beginning to die inside. Then I remembered why I joined the organization in the first place, my promise to write this book, and my spirit came alive again with renewed vision.

In the Talmud there is a saying: "When the student is ready, the teacher appears." Sometimes the teacher can come in the form of a book. Quite by accident, I stumbled upon a 25-year-old book at a garage sale. For 50 cents, I bought *Atlas Shrugged*, written by Ayn Rand in 1957. After reading the first few pages, I could not put it down. It grabbed me by the throat and changed my life.

The devastatingly captivating novel is about brilliant, passionate people and their struggles with bureaucracy. The main characters, after exhausting all possibilities of satisfying their own sense of mission, passion and desire for excellence, tire of the organizational insanity they encounter and take their intelligence and spirit elsewhere.

Before too long, all of the brilliance leaves and the corporations crumble. Forty years later, I was seeing this phenomenon—this stifling of spirit by bureaucracy—still happening. This had happened to David and it was happening to me. Why? And what could we do about it?

When people are passionate about their work, their life force energy—their spirit—is engaged. They sense a broader, deeper meaning in their work, a greater purpose, a calling to leave a legacy, to make a contribution to something bigger. For example, they want to make this world a better place, improve the lives of others or assist in the evolution of the human soul.

When people join a corporation, do they do so for more than money? Do they join because they see a greater possibility of fulfilling their mission in life, of making a difference in partnership with someone or something bigger, an organization whose mission matches their own? This book says that they do. This book is about, and for, those people.

The human spirit has the power to overcome great obstacles and help people soar. Leaders have choices. They can engage the spirit, ignore it, or dampen it. Countless books on library shelves tell us that productivity goes up when employees are passionate about what they do, when their spirit is engaged. Yet corporate cultures often force people in power to control the human spirit, to manage it. In so doing, somehow, they dampen it. Peters and Waterman told us in their 1982 book, *In Search of Excellence*, that most organizations "take a negative view of their people."

> They verbally berate their employees for poor performance . . . . They call for risk taking but punish even tiny failures. They want innovation but kill the spirit of the champion . . . . They design systems that seem calculated to tear down their workers' self-image. They might not mean to be doing that but they are.

We knew this 15 years ago. Indeed we knew it 50 years ago. We are trying to do things differently, those of us who work in, or write about, organizations. We are trying to nourish the idealism of our passionate employees because we know that it is good both for them and for the company. Perhaps we are getting better at encouraging spirit in the workplace, but something is still missing. This is what I call organizational insanity—that craziness that tells us that passion is good for the bottom line, that leads us to seek it out and hire it, then, once we have it, to stanch it. We consciously and unconsciously put out the fires in the hearts of our employees, cause misery and invariably waste money in lost productivity. This book deals with how we do it, why we do it, how people can deal with it when it is done to them, and how we can begin to behave differently at all levels of our organizations.

The first four chapters describe the results of extensive personal interviews that I conducted with 20 people, who had experience at a variety of levels in more than 50 organizations employing anywhere from 50 to 40,000 people. I asked them four clusters of questions: First, when they began their jobs, was their spirit engaged? Did they have a vision, a calling, a desire, indeed conviction to make a difference? Second, was their spirit engaged now? If not, what happened, what discouraged or dampened their spirit. Third, how did they cope? What did they do? Did they try to get their spirit back? Did they succeed? Lastly, what advice do they have for us? What would have sustained, indeed nourished their spirit, their passion for their work?

The last chapter of the book probes why this is still happening in organizations today. If we know that passionate employees, those whose spirit is engaged, are more productive, why and how do we keep dampening them? How can we begin to choose a different path?

Within the pages of this book are some of these answers. There are suggestions for employees who feel their spirit is being dampened, as well as examples of unhealthy and healthy ways of coping. There are tips for supervisors, managers and leaders on how to nourish and keep alive the passion, the spirit of their employees, the lifeblood that keeps their organization vibrant.

If, through this book, even one life is improved, one illness is prevented, one human spirit is renewed, then the interviewing, writing and publishing will all have been worthwhile. Human life, indeed the life force inside each human, is made of stuff bigger than all of us. It is a spark of the universal life force, of a higher power, of God, and to squander it or squash it, is blasphemy.

In The Beginning

Engaged Spirit

This book is about spirit, engaged spirit, and a spirited workforce. It is not about religion, or values or ethics or moral codes. If you read this book, I guarantee, you will *not* learn how to meditate.

Then what do I mean by the word spirit? What am I saying when I write of a person's spirit being engaged? What is a spirited workforce? And why would anyone want such a workforce anyway? Let us begin the answer with a story.

My daughter Cynthia always struggled with mathematics. Times tables eluded her to the point where, at age 21, she still added the numbers up. For example, in her mind, it looked like this: 6x6 was 6+6+6+6+6+6. She passed high-school math through sheer grit, hard work and lots of tears and frustration, pledging never to do math without a calculator again as long as she lived.

I always encourage my children to follow their dreams—to find out what their special purpose is on this earth, what nourishes their soul, what interests them so much that they could keep working on it until 3 a.m. without noticing the time. I believe that is what adolescence is for, to experiment and find out who we are and why we are here. Too many of us do not get around to this until we are in our 40s. Then we sometimes feel compelled to leave lucrative jobs, marriages, family and friends to "find ourselves."

Cynthia's passion is photography. It is more than a love. Through it, she can bring beauty and truth to others. Cynthia sees things that others cannot, and she brings that vision to the world. At college, Cynthia is learning to become a professional photographer. As part of her program, last term she had to take chemistry and physics, both of which involved advanced mathematics. The tears and fears, as she registered last year and saw this on the course list, seemed endless. She felt sure her future as a photographer would go up in smoke.

Final exams came. She did well in physics. In chemistry, she did fabulously. She scored a perfect 100 per cent. Did Cynthia all of a sudden develop some new brain cells? I do not think so. The impossible math became quite possible when it had meaning that was linked with what Cynthia saw as her mission in life.

So when I give my talks on surviving organizational transitions and finding new careers, I say: "It is not the number of brain cells, it is your spirit that moves you." If Cynthia could get 100 per cent in chemistry, anything is possible.

When I talk about spirit, I am referring to a life-force energy inside each of us, a spark, perhaps, of the divine—an energy that gives our life meaning, purpose, and keeps us motivated and positive about life and the role or contribution we have to make.

When I ask if a person's spirit is engaged I mean: What are you here for? Why are you on this planet? Is it to have a mortgage, two kids and liver paté rotting in the fridge? I do not think so. Perhaps in our 20s we had those objectives. If we were lucky enough to accomplish them, what happened? Many of us found life empty. We have discovered that life is about more than acquisitions. It is about who we are and what we are here for. It is about looking back on our lives from our deathbed and saying: "I was my best. I used the gifts that I was fortunate enough to be born with."

The world is different because each and every one of us is here. If we are worrying about what we will do with our lives, we can stop worrying because we have already begun our mission with our first breath. Like when we throw a pebble into a lake, and it causes ripples and affects whatever it touches, so does our every move, our every word, our every deed have profound effects. Something that seems as simple as being a person who smiles easily and often can have enormous positive effect on others. People with very little formal education, who do not make a lot of money and do not think their jobs are very noble, can affect more people more positively than they know, simply by smiling. And conversely, people in traditionally highly regarded professions, such as medicine, can undermine excellent medical treatment with a cold, unpleasant, distant attitude.

We cannot escape it. Our mere existence makes a difference. How much of a difference is up to us. This is where spirit comes in. When our spirit is engaged in what we do, and we are conscious about it, our potential to influence the world and the people in it in positive ways can increase exponentially.

What do I mean when I say that a person's spirit is engaged? Think, for a moment, about a bicycle. Sometimes when we shift gears, the chain rattles for a moment then it clicks in and we take off. When I speak of spirit being engaged, I mean like the gears on a bicycle, clicked in place, giving us power. Conversely, when the chain comes off, one can pedal forever and not get very far.

Sometimes I see people in health clubs riding stationary bicycles. I know quite a few people who do this for fitness and health. They are improving their heart and muscles. It is not unusual for some people to leave work at lunch to spend half an hour on a stationary bicycle. Could this not also be a metaphor for many of us *at* work? We go through life riding our bicycle in place, not getting where we could be going because our chain is not clicked in. We go through the motions. We put in time. Our spirit is not engaged. We go through our days like zombies.

When we take the time to think about who we are and why we are here, and then we seek work that fulfils that purpose, our spirit is engaged in our work. The work has meaning. Our life has meaning. The two become inextricably intertwined.

When I speak of a spirited workforce, I mean a workforce that consists of people whose spirits are engaged. They *care* about their work because it means something to them. It is through their work, and in partnership with their organization, that they hope to make a difference, to leave a legacy. Through the door of this partnership, perhaps in one way, lies their immortality.

Why would anyone want a spirited workforce? We come full circle, back to Cynthia. Look at her increased ability! Look at her productivity! Believe me, Cynthia is not unique. The people I spoke with believed they were far more productive when their spirits were engaged. Which kind of person would you want working for you?

The People

I moved from Toronto, a vibrant growing business center, to Ottawa, a lovely four-season city nestled among rivers, near mountains, with cross-country skiing and cycling minutes from home. On weekends, the city is vibrant with recreational life, with festivals all year round, and entire families enjoying the outdoors regardless of the cold weather, which has been known to reach -35°C in the winter. But come 8:30 a.m. Monday, these very same people seem to turn into zombies, as if they had an "off" switch controlling their human spirit. Their pace and productivity slow to a fraction of what it had been on the weekend. I found the contrast astounding. Is work, by definition, something one must dislike and do in slow motion? What invisible force was causing this? Did these people *want* to be this way? What kept them in this condition? Could their spirit for work be turned on again, or were they content to keep it turned off forever? Was this a public-sector phenomenon, since Ottawa, the capital of Canada, has thousands of federal public servants? In attempting to answer these questions, I went far beyond Ottawa and interviewed people working in organizations in various cities in Canada and the United States.

I conducted thorough, in-depth interviews with 20 people who had experience in more than 50 different organizations. They were currently living in Montreal, Toronto, Ottawa, New York City, Detroit, and Ann Arbor, Michigan. There were 11 men and nine women. Most people were between the ages of 38 to 50, with two in their 60s and one in his early 30s. Five people were professional or technical specialists who worked within organizations, but essentially on their own. Fifteen of the people had some degree of responsibility over others, ranging from first-level supervisory to senior management. All but one had some post-secondary education. Interestingly, the person who held the most senior, most responsible position of all those interviewed, had the least formal education. Ten people came from the public sector, 10 from the private sector. The number of employees in the organizations in which these people worked ranged from 50 to more than 40,000.

They came from many different walks of life. The people I spoke with included a nurse, a Native elder, four government bureaucrats, two adult educators, a biologist, a computer specialist, an aircraft technician, two psychologists, a university professor, a social worker, a secretary, an air traffic controller, a buyer for a major corporation, a banker and an insurance agent turned minister.

The Passion

I asked them: When you started in your job with this organization, was your spirit engaged? Did you have a sense of mission, a feeling that you could make a difference? Without exception, they all responded affirmatively. They said that they were passionate about what they could accomplish. They felt they could make a difference.

All of them wanted to make the world a better place. They wanted to improve on something so others would benefit. It is what they wanted to improve that is fascinating. Not one of these people was looking for personal financial gain. They certainly wanted to earn enough to keep food on the table, but not one of them mentioned making money or having financial security as something that fuelled their passion. These were not people who were going to go out into the world, build their own business, develop better widgets and make millions. The mission they spoke of was inextricably linked to their role in their organization. They wanted to make the world a better place through and in partnership with their organization. These were company people. Their work could only be meaningful within the organization, not out on their own. They came on board because they sensed that there was a match between their mission and the mission of the organization.

Their passion and spirit are captured in the following quotations:

"I want to discover *truth* and share it with the world."

—*university professor*

"I want to give disadvantaged youth and adults a chance for a decent education."

—*adult educator*

"I have this passion to create perfect, safe airplanes."

—*aircraft technician*

"We treat our elderly with disrespect. I want to do my best to give them the very best care possible."

—*nurse*

"Pollution and human carelessness are killing our planet. My mission is to save the world from environmental destruction."

—*biologist*

"I work at solving the complicated multi faceted problems involved in child-abuse situations. I want to make a difference, to have a positive impact on peoples lives."

—*social worker*

"There are far too many First Nations people in prisons. This is because they have lost contact with their spirituality. I want to bring Native spirituality through ritual and ceremony to First Nations people in prison, to prevent them from returning to prison over and over again."

—*Mic Mac elder*

"I want to repay my immigrant parents' debt to this country by making a contribution to Canada."

—*government bureaucrat*

All of these people joined organizations whose goals matched their own. They thought they could better achieve their life's mission in partnership with these organizations. They were passionate about their work. As Yenta, the matchmaker, from the Broadway musical *Fiddler on the Roof*, would say, "What a match!"

What Turns The Spirit Off?

What happened to these people whose spirit was so well matched with the mission of the organization? What happened to these potentially powerful, productive unions?

I asked: Do you still have this sense of mission today? Is your spirit still engaged at work? If not, how long did it last? What were the factors that changed it? What happened at work that encouraged or dampened your sense of mission?

Unfortunately, every one of the people interviewed, every one of these wonderfully passionate company people felt that their spirit had been dampened. They all described feelings of being emotionally and mentally battered. In most of the cases, it happened within the first six months. It took a very short time for these people to realize that there was no way that they would be enabled to do what they thought they had been hired for. Their problems fell into three categories: Direction, Bureaucracy and Relationship with their Boss.

Deleterious Direction

Sometimes, the actions of the senior management team or a particular person in charge dampened the spirit of the employee or groups of employees. Senior managers dampened peoples' spirits with three kinds of behaviour: Apathy, Indecision, and Vacillating Vision.

Apathy

Sometimes employees got the impression that no one on the senior management team cared whether any work was done or not.

Mark was one of our four career bureaucrats. He had joined the federal government right after university. He wanted to write legislation to ensure that the laws were fair and respected individuals as well as groups of people. He had worked for many different departments and on different types of legislation. He worked on teams in conjunction with employees, union representatives, management and lawyers. He held consultations with various sectors of departmental employees and the public to ensure extensive and fair consultation on each piece of policy or legislation he participated in developing.

In one particular case, he was part of a team working on a very politically sensitive project. The team worked diligently but kept getting mixed signals from the people in charge. It often seemed as if no one was at the helm. "They just kept giving us their approval and allowing us to go on, although they never seemed to care whether we accomplished our objectives or not. It was as if no one had the guts to suggest that we stop and take a look at this." It was a case of the "Abilene Paradox," described in the book by Jerry Harvey.

The *Abilene Paradox,* which is about corporate decision-making, describes a scene from the author's childhood. The family was sitting on the porch sipping lemonade on a hot, dusty Texas day, when one family member suggested a trip to Abilene for lunch in the air-conditioned cafeteria. It was only after one and half hours in a hot, dusty car, an inedible lunch and one and a half hot, dusty hours back, that the family members discovered that not one of them had actually wanted to go in the first place. They had been perfectly happy on the porch sipping lemonade, but not one of them wanted to be obstructionist by saying that the trip was a lousy idea.

In the corporate scenario experienced by Mark, it seemed as if senior management was unable to make a concrete decision. The words were, "go ahead." But the message was, "We do not care whether you get there or not."

What is most fascinating about lack of clear direction from senior management, is that the process can go even further up the line. In this particular case, a member of the senior management team was also interviewed. As it turned out, the team had its hands tied as well, being at the mercy of political forces. The senior management team itself was experiencing the same lack of clarity and direction from above and was therefore unable to give clear direction to the people below.

This was a very difficult situation and it was not that senior management did not know what to do, it was that they were frozen in time until certain events took place in the political arena. They too, had their spirits dampened. Unfortunately, the non-verbal communication received by the team below them was, "We really don't care."

Indecision

Two other government bureaucrats, **Patty** and **Jack**, told how a single senior manager had a great impact on the lives of more than 900 employees by stalling a planned reorganization for almost a year. Patty and Jack worked in different parts of the same division of which this senior manager was the head. The division was going to be divided and moving in very distinct directions. In addition, the group had to be downsized by one third. The uncertainties were creating anxiety and depressing morale.

About one third of the employees, because of the nature of their work, were reasonably clear where they would be going. Six months into the process, a meeting was held for all middle and senior managers (fiftysomething people). Jack was invited, Patty was not. According to Jack, it was clear by the lack of participation, the dour faces around the room and the lack of small talk, that although these people were there in body, their spirits were already gone.

Because of his position on the management team, Jack knew that the senior manager was being pressured by boss, peers and the management team below, to let the people go. The longer they stayed, the lower productivity got. In addition, people were having to physically move their offices and undergo a temporary reorganization, which many felt was made redundant by the upcoming larger reorganization. Yet the senior manager would not halt the temporary moves, thereby forcing additional perceived unnecessary stress onto an already stressed-to-the-limit population. Jack felt powerless. He had to carry out the senior manager's orders. Patty was even more powerless because she was lower on the organizational chart.

At first, both Jack and Patty observed, productivity slowed because people were angry. They were also having extreme difficulty coping with the new, temporary organizational structure, which not only moved people but also split formerly well-functioning teams into separate groups reporting up the line to two people who were in a power war. To complicate matters, because the reorganization was temporary, appropriate time was never taken to sort out who did what and to whom. People who had worked together beautifully for years ended up hating each other. Eventually, people got tired of the insanity and disengaged. By six months into the project, people were resigned to waiting it out, taking extra vacation, and moving on slow speed until the time for the real reorganization came. Unfortunately, by that time, very few people cared any more about the organization and its mission. All that seemed important was that they were really angry with the senior manager. People started scrambling to find other jobs and invested their energy in themselves and their careers, allowing a poorly functioning organization to fall even farther apart. People had to take care of themselves. Unable to do it in synchrony with the organization, they did it alone. Said Jack, "The senior manager charged ahead to the beat of a single drummer, alone."

Vacillating Vision

Another way in which senior management was perceived to dampen people's spirits was by making decisions and changing direction too quickly and not giving employees time to adjust. These were often referred to as "waves of changes." Employees reported that they were just regaining their balance when they were smacked with another huge wave.

Anne, an adult educator, had always held very strong political beliefs. Unexpectedly, her political party, the underdog, got into power. She saw this as a dream come true. She wanted to work for them. She saw the opportunity to do so much for other people. She became part of a "powerful and passionate team." She called it "the chance of a lifetime." Unfortunately, the dream soon turned into a nightmare. She said: "There were dozens of small blows all the time. Our team would go away for a two-day strategic planning retreat, make plans and come back euphoric, only to have all our plans dashed when we got home. Our projects would be cancelled, our decisions overridden by higher ups . . . . We had made promises to clients that we were unable to keep. We felt that we had no control, no input and were not valued. It seemed as if there was no commitment from upstairs. There was such bureaucratic uncertainty and constant unplanned change from the top that we could never get any work done. We spent most of our time preparing for and adjusting to the changes. People were just worn down."

Ellen, a buyer with a large organization, had a similar experience. "We went through a major reorganization last year," she said. "It involved a huge amount of work, but we saw the value of it, all pitched in, rolled up our sleeves and got it done. Last Monday, senior management announced a complete reorganization once again. I skipped the denial stage and went straight to anger. I just cannot go through this again. We finally got things working and now we have to break them up again."

Clearly what **Mark, Patty, Jack, Anne** and **Ellen** needed from senior management was not only clear direction, but also commitment. The vacillating of the senior management team, its inability to either make decisions on clear directions or stick with one direction long enough for anything to get accomplished, had devastating effects on their employees.

Rigid Rules

The most common complaint that people had about how their spirit got dampened involved the people above them following the letter rather than the spirit of a certain law, thereby causing unmeasurable harm to employee morale, the project employees were working on and in some cases, even public safety and health.

We create rules in order to serve us, to make our lives run smoother and easier. Unfortunately, once rules are in place they sometimes become our master. Rules, in some cases, can become more important than the people they were created to serve. Back in the 1960s, the folk-singing group, The Kingston Trio, sang a satirical song called *MTA*, about a subway fare increase on the Massachusetts Transit authority. To ride the MTA trains, passengers paid once when they got on and again when they got off. Poor Charlie, being short of just one nickel at the end of his ride, was doomed to stay on the train for the rest of his life.

Sean had a passion for airplanes. He wanted to build perfect planes and therefore studied aircraft technology and got a job as a technician with a small airline. His job, which he took very seriously, was to repair small aircraft. His training put him in a position to know which airplanes were safe and which were not. Expensive repairs were often required to render an airplane safe. The small company, struggling to stay in business, sometimes had to let certain repairs wait. By his standards, planes that should not have been in the air went up anyway.

He felt that airplane inspection and maintenance were not taken seriously enough at this company. They were too expensive. He became a crusader for safety, referred to by some as a troublemaker. According to the rules, it was not his job to inspect airplanes. His job was to fix what he was told to fix, *period*! Inspectors inspect aircraft and file reports. Technicians fix aircraft and keep their mouths shut.

One day, two of his pilot friends were to be sent up in a plane that he knew had a cracked engine casing. He said: "I was told by both my supervisor and the owner of the company to keep my big mouth shut. I called the chief pilot and told him. The plane was taken off the line and I was taken off the job."

Florence is a registered nurse who wanted to improve the way we treat our elderly in North American society. Her mission was to give quality, loving care to people in their final, declining years. She got a job as head of nursing in a personal care home.

The rules that dampened her spirit were those concerning the deference given to doctors, even when health and safety were at stake. Nurses were terrified to break the rules for fear of being intimidated and yelled at by medical staff. One case was indelibly etched in her mind. Local doctors who provided on-call service and were required to officially pronounce death, were not to be disturbed at home for any reason whatsoever after 10 p.m. One night, an elderly patient was found dead in her bed at 10:15. Florence was flabbergasted to learn when she arrived at work the next morning that her staff, well socialized to obey the rules at all costs, would not disturb the doctor at home to have him come in and declare the person officially dead so that they could notify the family. The woman was left in the bed until morning, even though three other patients shared the room.

Florence complained that this was unfair and insensitive to the family and also to the other patients in the room, especially since the expired patient was emitting a foul odour. She was simply told to open the window.

Crusading for the rights of patients and their families in the face of unreasonable rules at first dampened her spirit, then got her labelled a troublemaker and eventually got her fired.

Russell, a biologist, is an environmentalist with a passion to help save the world from polluting itself into oblivion. He left a consulting firm to join a larger bureaucracy, hoping for a chance to save the world in a bigger way.

Within six months, he started receiving criticism for such petty things as putting his time sheet on his boss's desk instead of in his mail box, and for filling it in with Xs instead of check marks.

Scientific reports had to be rewritten *ad nauseam*. The objective was to say what his boss perceived senior management wanted to hear, not what the facts were. He called it a technical and political cover-your-behind exercise. He was astounded at the time spent rewriting one-page memos and debating who to carbon copy and who not.

He had come from a consulting firm where technical expertise and getting things done on time and within budget were valued. Here there was lots of time, which seemed to be devoted to empire building and playing the game. When he was an external consultant, this same organization would pay him to do a certain report. Now, as an internal consultant doing the same project and report that he would have been doing from the outside, he was suddenly, because of the rules, a "small frog in a big puddle." He was no longer allowed to make decisions as a person. A whole hierarchy of people was needed to review his work. "There were blanks to be filled in on the reports such as prepared by, reviewed by, approved by, etc., *ad nauseam*." He said: "They treat me like a child and I have an MSc in biology. We must follow the rules and cover the organization's butt even if it means killing the fish and destroying the forests."

Sean, **Florence** and **Russell** were astounded to find that the rules were more important than the people or the environment. Where were these people's values? Perhaps the organizations had good reason for creating and enforcing these rules. The main reasons described above, however, seemed to be fear and saving money. In all three cases, Sean, Florence and Russell felt that by following the letter rather than the spirit of the law, public safety and health were endangered.

Bothered Bosses

The last group is composed almost exclusively of specialists working in organizations that send out double messages. These people were hired because they had a high level of knowledge or expertise in a certain area. Their bosses then found them, it seems, very difficult to "keep in line."

People drew upon relatively forceful language when describing their experiences in this category. They used words such as "battered," "humiliated" and "belittled." It was as if they experienced someone above them having a strong need to put them in their proper place. Something about these people—their level of knowledge and skill, their confidence in themselves, their innovation, perhaps their creativity—provoked severely negative, almost jealous reactions from their bosses. It seemed as if these people, who perceived themselves as creative, innovative risk takers, were hired to take the organization to a new level and then, when they did, their bosses got scared and tried to stop them, or at least slow them down.

Let us take a few moments to look at the sorts of things that happened to create this feeling of being battered, of having one's spirit dampened.

Susan is a university professor who has more than 25 years experience and is world renowned in her field. She is a scholar who believes that her mission is to discover truth and share it with the world. She said: "My boss sees me as a superstar who must be managed. There is no money for me to go to local conferences, yet my colleagues get to travel out of the country. I am the most productive person in the department, with four books and more than 60 articles published, and he gives me a bad performance appraisal, putting in writing that I should learn to manage my husband."

Noel is a Native elder. He is passionate about bringing native spirituality, through ritual and ceremony, back to the people, particularly those in trouble with addictions or in prison. He was hired on contract to bring Native spirituality to First Nations inmates across the country because research has shown that returning to Native spiritual ways can reduce recidivism.

The senior manager who originally hired Noel was extremely supportive of the concept of Native spirituality. Noel was invited to management meetings and consulted on all issues involving Native inmates. Then, management changed. The new people were less enamored with Native spirituality.

Noel was not told about critical meetings and was excluded from the information loop. He felt belittled, silenced, and not valued by authorities who seemed to be uncomfortable with his knowledge, his intelligence and his threat to the status quo.

Sarah, a psychologist, was committed to helping people in organizations by diminishing organizational stress. Her boss was an old-style manager who was both commanding and controlling. At times, she was convinced he would have been more suited to running a dog-obedience school rather than a personnel department. Sarah felt that there was a continuous and systematic destruction of her credibility as a professional. "Nothing I said had value, was of interest, or was correct. My role was to sit in the corner and be quiet. I was like a fly that he wished would just go away, and not cause trouble by saying anything innovative. I would say things and he would scrunch up his face as if I was speaking another language. Instead of trying to understand what I was talking about, he would shut me down. He undermined my self-esteem by attacking my personality, even my facial expressions and tone of voice. I began to feel as if I was so inadequate that I should just sit in a corner and be silent, since I obviously did not know how to behave in public."

Other people spoke of similar experiences, but with a succession of bosses over a longer period of time. Three people were hired to develop programs that were new to the organization. In the beginning, while senior management still knew little about the programs, these people enjoyed a honeymoon phase. Part of their role was to educate management. However, as the bosses got educated, and started to see the potential impact of these programs, they reacted by putting up barriers. Suddenly there were bureaucratic fights at every turn. There was intense resistance to the new programs. The programs were seen as different, unknown, scary and therefore unnecessary, even though these individuals were originally hired to implement them. As **Ernie,** a psychologist noted, "There were the little nos and the big nos. It was a constant and seemingly never-ending political battle." He saw a large part of his work as understanding the fabric of the "wall" and determining where the weak spots were. It was as if these individuals had been hired to run, were expected to do so with their feet tied together, and were then criticized for not running properly. The negativity further took the form of criticism in public, abject avoidance and poor performance appraisals.

In all of the above cases, poor performance appraisals were a particular problem since they often had the effect of holding the employee prisoner in the job. As long as the bosses succeeded in convincing the employees that they were inadequate and told the employees they were prepared to tell the world about it, the employees felt trapped. Then the bosses convinced the employees to stay until they improved, which of course they could never do under the prevailing conditions.

Susan, **Noel**, **Sarah**, and **Ernie** had expertise in areas that their bosses did not. Rather than encouraging them to soar, it seemed to these people that their bosses did everything in their power to slow them down.

Summary

So, with all of the people I interviewed, the things that dampened their spirit, that caused it to disengage, fell into three main categories. Although there may have been some overlap, the primary reason each person mentioned fell into one of the three areas mentioned above: senior management's lack of direction, bureaucratic structure and rules, and unhealthy relationships with immediate supervisors.

In order to keep spirit alive, people need clear, direct, committed corporate direction from senior management. They need the rules to be more elastic, particularly when health and safety are at stake. Last, they need to be managed by someone who is not afraid of them or their knowledge—someone who can let, indeed encourage them, to soar.

Survival Strategies

Is the human spirit a renewable resource? When it is exhausted or dampened, does it go away and die, or is it a driving force that continues to resurface? Is the requirement to keep the spirit alive a compelling human need such as hunger or thirst?

I left my job in Toronto, sold my home, and singlehandedly relocated my three daughters aged 9, 14 and 16, my dog and my stress management cat (he makes me relax) to a new city. I bought a new home, enrolled my daughters in new schools and helped them adjust to a place that had more snow and more French than they had ever seen or heard in their lives. I did all of this because my spirit was engaged. I did not move only because there was a little more money, or because Ottawa is a smaller city with a gentler pace. I moved because I had a calling. In my job interview, I told them about what I wanted to do in organizations. I thought that was what got me hired. Wrong!

There I was, running an expanded employee assistance program for an organization employing more than 20,000 people. A network of psychologists and social workers across the country looked to me for professional advice and direction. Their mandate included providing individual counselling to employees who had personal problems that were affecting their work performance. They also provided advice to managers, delivered seminars and led organizational development initiatives. My role included providing advice and resource material to the counsellors, maintaining national statistics, and advising senior management on all counselling-related issues. I had a Ph.D. in Adult Education and Psychology and knew, or so I thought, a lot about communication, adult learning, relationships, and other things of that nature. In less than six months, I realized that I would not be allowed to do anything that I had dreamed of doing.

I soon noticed, since I collated the statistics for the country, that what I had experienced in the field in Toronto was happening across the country. What was bringing people to the counsellors' doors, much of the time, was neither substance abuse nor family problems. It was organizational issues. Yet my advice, although I offered it, was not welcome on these matters. Every time I ventured outside what was narrowly defined as my area of expertise, I got into trouble with my boss. On a couple of occasions, he actually did seek my advice for specific cases. But for larger group organizational issues, for some reason, I was not considered a competent source for advice.

Each year, I would list my goals and objectives. At appraisal time, although my goals and objectives were well exceeded, a major personality "flaw" would be discovered that overshadowed all the accomplishments. In four years, I never figured out what my supervisor wanted of me, ever. My major mistake was in not leaving after the first six months.

Another of my mistakes was my persistence. I always look for the flaws inside myself, how I can improve. I always give the other person the benefit of the doubt. I would listen carefully to my supposed character or personality flaw and do my best to correct it, only to be confronted the next year with some new one. His favorite theme was that I had poor communication skills. After the second year of this, I was ready to lodge a harassment complaint. Miraculously, the situation began to turn around.

My boss did not have the best reputation as a people person. He was known to be a hard-line command and control, no-nonsense manager. One argued with this man at one's peril. I knew this about him in advance, but I went to work for him anyway because I respected his forthrightness. He said it like it was. I thought I could handle gruffness as long as it was honest. Honesty was not the issue. This man was working hard and doing his best. He actually thought he was a good communicator. He did not know what he did not know. As far as I could tell, his definition of a good communicator or facilitator differed from most other people's.

When I attended my first management retreat, I saw trouble ahead. No one uttered a word. Everyone eyed each other suspiciously. People back-stabbed, seeking the boss's favor. All "real" talk happened in washrooms and corridors during the breaks. People smiled in his presence, did as they were told, kept their mouths shut and did their best to deflect any of his anger onto someone else. It felt like bad kindergarten. I told myself I was a specialist in this area. I had to *do* something about this.

During my first year, when he asked for input from all participants on forthcoming management retreats, I made suggestions about process; how to improve communication with and among the team; how to run the retreats in ways that encouraged participation and lessened the fear. I sought to change the back-stabbing, competitive, counterproductive dynamics. I discussed it ever so gently, because to call a spade a spade would have cost me my job and I had three children to support. In retrospect, perhaps I could have been more forthright, but I was frightened.

I offered to lead seminars, suggested consultants and recommended books. Nothing happened. I was just another member of the team so he would not let me help him or my peers by designing process or facilitating retreats. Outside consultants had to be brought in, sometimes at great cost, to do what I could have done for free. Although it drove me crazy, I still did not leave.

At management retreats, my colleagues would implore me with hound-dog eyes from across the room, to *do* something when the specially hired consultant was missing the point or boring us to death. Fool that I was, I would ask a question or make a point. Even though I intervened in a manner that I knew from my training was quite acceptable group process, I was invariably chastised afterward by my supervisor for being "selfish." Eventually, I stopped opening my mouth, too. What was the point?

One day my boss happened to mention that he played a musical instrument. I coaxed and cajoled him into bringing his instrument to the next management retreat. I promised I would bring my guitar. We arrived early. As the managers began to arrive from across the country, they entered the lounge only to see him playing music. The expressions on their faces were priceless. To this day, I wish I had had a camera. One by one, they joined in the sing-along. So did the senior manager who came later.

A paradigm shift occurred that night. The team saw the human side of the boss. From then on, I brought my guitar to all retreats (twice per year for three more years). To this day, I do not know whether any of the other managers, including my boss, know that I was not singing for fun. This was the *only* vehicle I had for changing the culture. However, it amounted to only about three per cent of what I could have done if I had not been blocked by the powers that be.

In the interim, to keep myself sane, and also because my self-esteem was too low to search for another job, I began to work on this book on the side. As I did interviews and found out about other people's struggles, I began to feel less alone and more valuable. As the data emerged, my spirit began to recharge. I had found a place for my other 97 per cent.

Finally, my boss left the organization. I got a new boss who supported and encouraged me. I was allowed, finally, to design and deliver a seminar on Surviving Transition (Psychological First Aid) to a small group of people. It was such a success that I became very popular as a seminar leader with various organizations outside of my own. I had delivered seminars to thousands of people, before word got around in my own organization. Finally, after five years, I was asked to lead a seminar for one of our management retreats. Fifty of my peers from across the country and all the senior managers were there. They walked into the room with oh-no-what-are-we-in-for eyes. After about three minutes, people's jaws fell open. "My goodness," they said later, "we have never seen you in your element. We did not know you could do that." Amazing! I had been trying to show them for five years!

But it was too late. I had finally, 10 months after the departure of my previous boss, gotten my self-esteem back. My spirit was re-engaged and I had absolutely no trouble finding a new job.

Laced throughout my story are the three main ways people cope. These three categories represent various levels of disengagement of the spirit from the mission of the organization and re-engagement elsewhere. There are the fighters, the perception changers and the zombies at work.

Fighters

As I did, *all* people interviewed for this book tried at first to change the system. They were all fighters at the beginning. They fought to keep their passion alive, to change the bureaucracy, to stretch the rules, to influence senior management, to convince their bosses of whatever they needed to in order to continue doing what they thought they had been hired for. The fighters kept the battle going longer than the others, indeed, they kept fighting until they burned out.

In some ways, a person in this category is like a puppy who attaches itself to a pant leg and will not let go. These people would not give up. They kept fighting the corporate battles, and indeed, paving the way for others to follow. They treated being able to accomplish their mission as a fighting match: sometimes sparing, sometimes stepping back, ever inching forward.

The spirit of these people wasted away until they burned out. Exhausted and spent, they then split into two groups. The first group moved on. They accepted lateral transfers to other parts of the company, or other companies, accepting *anything* in order to get out. **Ernie,** the psychologist, said: "I left because to get the program to the next step would take more time and energy than I was willing to give. The constant struggle of trying to keep them onside got exhausting. After 27 times, it takes someone with more zest."

In some cases, it took a couple of transfers and a few years for these people to find new corporate homes, but they are now happy at work and their spirits are engaged.

A few others are in the middle of this process. They have one foot on the dock and one foot on the boat. They are keeping their spirits alive and themselves sane by spending evenings and weekends investing in hobbies; for example, water-colour painting, training a new puppy, gardening, or reading novels while they decide what to do. Although many people invest in hobbies, this group was different in that they expressly described the hobby as a form of therapy, something constant to focus on to capture their spirit while they decided on what to do at work. **Mary**, the computer specialist, said: "I paint like crazy on the weekends. At work, I continue to fight for what I believe is right. People are burning out like crazy. The brains are leaving and the company is getting a bad name. There is malaise all around and people are not happy at work any more. I am re-evaluating what to do with the rest of my life. I may make a big career change. "

The other group of people in the fighter category also kept on trying until they burned out, but they left not of their own choice. A cataclysmic event happened and they snapped, causing them to say, "*no way*." They were then fired or bought out.

Sean, the airplane technician, said: "I would play their game of denial. I would tell myself it would be OK—to relax and not be such a perfectionist." Finally, as described earlier, he stood up to management once too many times and was fired. What does he do now? He still has his sense of mission: to build perfect airplanes. But he builds perfect *model* airplanes as a hobby. As a job, he has changed careers and become a landscape architect. He says: "You can be a perfectionist with flowers and nobody dies!"

Noel, the Native elder, asked for two meetings to discuss the situation. He was criticized, belittled and felt that none of his ideas was valued. Then a sacred sweat lodge that the inmates had built on the prison grounds was bulldozed, allegedly by accident. Noel then realized he was wasting his time. He stopped fighting. He said he "left gently, stood back respectfully," allowing his contract to be terminated and not pushing for renewal.

Florence, the nurse in the personal care home, said she "shut up and went with the flow." She did as she was told for as long as she could, but people's lives were at stake. She said: "I couldn't stand it any more. Certain things, for example, a drug error could not be hidden and had to be dealt with. I got the reputation of being a Jekyll and Hyde. I turned myself inside out trying to make it work. I spoke with the owners and with the chief of staff. I hired a consultant, spending $350 of my own money trying to problem-solve. When they refused to even discuss the situation with me, I knew my time was up."

Recognizing that her talents as a crusader were being wasted, Florence has redirected her fighting spirit and found a new mission in life that involves helping the planet in a larger way. In addition, she promotes a line of products that clean the environment and promote wellness. On the back burner simmers her dream to write books about care for the elderly and abused nurses.

Like I did in the first year, these people tried in various ways to change the situation in which they found themselves. In the end, they either gave up trying or were in the process of giving up, choosing to invest their energy in non-professional after-hours pursuits.

Tips For Fighters

For those of you who find yourselves in this category, it is really important to read the signposts. Life is not about being miserable. Sometimes we make a mistake. A little while ago, I adopted a homeless five-month-old black Labrador puppy. I soon found out why he was homeless. There is a fine line between high-spirited and nuts. This dog was nuts. In the second month, after six classes of obedience school, he pulled me over while walking and I smacked my head on the concrete sidewalk. I stumbled home, remaining conscious long enough for my daughter to get me to the hospital. I had blurred vision for four months. Two months after this fall, he suddenly darted in front of my bicycle, knocked me off and landed me in the hospital again with gravel road rash that took three weeks to heal. He is a lovable, adorable dog, but he was too much for me. He ate my couch, pulled my blinds off the window, soiled the carpet and terrified the cat. He took over my life. But I am smarter now. I do not bang my head against the wall anymore (usually). I found him a wonderful home in the country where he can run in the woods, swim in the lake and is not allowed anywhere near a carpet.

Do not bang your head against the wall! Do not keep fighting until you wind up in the hospital with a heart attack, ulcer, nervous breakdown or cancer! Find another job, or change your eyes.

Perception Changers

These people also fought the system at the beginning. The members of this group were different in that they either saw the writing on the wall *before* they burned out or caught themselves in the process of burning out, stopped and did something about it.

As Lao Tzu said in the *Tao Te Ching*: "When the winds of change blow, build windmills." These people did just that.

They changed what gave them meaning in their work. They altered what they took as signals that they were achieving their mission. They used the negative energy from their work to propel them into a new direction. These people began to rely on themselves, their internal barometer, to determine whether their work was meaningful. The people in this group coped by changing what they perceived as signs that they were accomplishing their mission in life. To illustrate this concept, let us return to our stories.

We spoke of **Mark** earlier. He was the project leader whose legislation writing was hamstrung by political forces that would not allow the senior management team to make a decision. When asked how he had coped during the times of managerial indecision, Mark had some very powerful things to say.

The most important thing that Mark did was that he made the decision not to tie his sense of achievement to the completion of the project. He had to get his feelings of accomplishment from something else. Management was undecided. If the only thing that would make him feel successful was total completion of the project, he could perhaps face the prospect of endless frustration and dampening of his spirit. His mission became to learn as much as possible and to make sure the project was done "right" according to his personal standards, that the aspects of the project that he worked on would be done thoroughly and with full client consultation.

The second thing that Mark did, rather than rely on managerial approval or recognition, was to have his team set up their own internal benchmarks. "We had to be self-driven. We created our own timetable, set tangible milestones, tied off pieces, knocked down one more barrier. This gave us a sense of achievement. Even if the project never went anywhere, we got satisfaction from the pieces we did, and the fact that we completed them in the best possible manner and on time."

Third, Mark attributed the survival of his mental health to the fact that he had a heathy skepticism about the project from the beginning, and also to the fact that it was a project that he knew would not go on forever. He made sure that he never lost sight of the light at the end of the tunnel, no matter how long the tunnel seemed at certain times.

As it turned out, the project was never completed. There was an election and a new government came into power. The legislation was never written. The team was disbanded. Mark, fortunately, had seen the writing on the wall and made a very timely career shift. He found a very satisfying job writing legislation somewhere else.

One of my favorite stories is about **George**. George was born of Croatian immigrant parents. He became a career federal civil servant because he wanted to make a contribution to Canada. George had gone back to school for a Master's degree. He had attended seven universities, taught at three of them, but felt that he was sadly underemployed. Like me, he felt he rarely, if ever, got a chance to use his knowledge on the job. Within a few months of beginning any position, he felt that his creativity was squashed by bureaucracy. No matter what he did or thought, like others in the previous chapter, he was hamstrung by the rules: what you could put on paper, who you were allowed to, or prevented from, talking to, and which information could be shared and with whom. He felt that he was in a little box that was way too small for his size.

Like Mark, George also survived by altering his perspective. He asked for lots of transfers and changed jobs frequently. He found things to enjoy in each job. Although his mission was to make a contribution to Canada, he developed secondary personal missions. He kept finding interesting work to do, seeking jobs with travel involved and applying for paid academic leave. He said: "I developed a personal secret that nobody at work knew. I do not work for government, I work for myself. What my boss thinks does not matter. I work for my own development, for the evolution of my own soul. I do my best so I will evolve. I have discovered a four-point survival strategy. First, I am in control of myself—how I think and how I feel. No one can control that, no matter what they do or say. Second, I stay out of office politics. I do not lose energy on something over which I have no control. Third, I take every opportunity I can on my own time to expand my knowledge, skills and understanding in every direction. I have a self-directed career. I never let the grass grow under my feet. If it is a slow time, I go to the library. Fourth, and most important, I develop, maintain and nurture a sense of humor at all times. I make it a giant game to reward myself."

Another way George has kept his spirit alive is by setting up, organizing and running a New Age association called Spiritual Frontiers Canada. He has been the mover and shaker behind this group, whose numbers are expanding exponentially. He arranges for guest speakers from all over Canada and the United States. He organizes discussions and social events for members and entertains them all by playing his accordion and flashing his huge smile. George keeps his own spirit alive.

My favorite part of the interview with George came at the end. We had spent a considerable amount of time talking about how his spirit had been dampened and how he had kept going. Clearly, both our spirits needed lightening at that moment. He then offered me a cup of tea and led me to the television set. He popped a cassette into the VCR and on the screen appeared two men and a woman singing opera, in *Croatian*!

I spent the next hour watching and listening to a musical comedy which he was kind enough to simultaneously translate. He told me this was one of his favorite videos because of its title and its message. Transliterated, the title is pronounced "Ko pyey-va zlo ney mis-lee." It means: "The one who sings thinks no evil." George hums a tune wherever he goes.

One more short example completes this section. **Russell,** the biologist, also changed his perspective. He managed his career in order to have more options. He became the manager of a large project so he could have more say. He tries to avoid being "stuck in a small box." He also works on the premise that forgiveness is easier to get than permission. He makes his own decisions about his project. He does not ask, he just does. He says: "If it turns out you were right, it waters down the criticism." He continues to speak up and be a risk-taker.

In addition, like many of the others, Russell has found outside outlets for his passion. He is a head Scout leader with five leaders under him. He says this prevents him from going crazy. It adds a feeling of "being in control" to his life and he is involved with nature, spending his time teaching people to love and care for it. He also belongs to many environmental organizations. He is being true to his values and his mission to save the environment.

Tips For Perception Changers

In order to keep your spirit alive at work, it is critical to change what you read as signs of your success. The people described in this section learned to set personal benchmarks for themselves and, in some cases, for their team. They placed value on continuing to grow, learn, acquire experience and on doing the best they could according to their own standards. They found joy and satisfaction both within and outside the job. Most important, they remembered to keep things in perspective and to laugh.

Zombies

The people in this category feel unable to leave their jobs just yet. They believe they cannot move because they think that they have nowhere to go at the moment. They perceive that they have two choices: either they die inside, or they find a way to achieve their mission and find meaning and recognition *outside* of the organization or the line of authority in which they find themselves.

This group is composed mostly of the last group in the previous chapter, the experts working inside an organization that telegraphs double messages about how it deals with them. Their superiors need them, but do not want to recognize them. In other words, they can be experts in everyone else's eyes but not in their boss's. Their bosses seem to need to keep them in line.

These people keep their spirit alive and get recognition outside of the organization by participating on committees, public speaking, and acquiring a string of publications. Most have become committed authors of books and articles and many of them speak at national and international conferences. When appraisal time comes around, they have ammunition. When their boss tries to tell them that they "are not a team player" or "have communication difficulties" or that "people do not like you" or that "your husband makes trouble", they have some real accomplishments they can show.

The big question is: Why have these people not rolled up their sleeping bag and moved on? Unfortunately, sometimes the negative perceptions of people in authority do strange things to one's own self-esteem. I know. It happened to me. For a while, many of these people actually believed that their bosses were right, that they had nothing tangible to offer, that they had personality flaws and that no other company would want them. Like me, they have since started to wake up.

Unfortunately for the organizations involved, these people will soon be on their way. In the interim, they make themselves scarce at work and they do as much as they can at home. Like the heros and heroines in Ayn Rand's novel *Atlas Shrugged* in the final stages before they left their organization, these people are giving the organization exactly what they think it wants from them, which is virtually nothing, and preparing for a career move. Just because the organization cannot seem to make use of the expertise it has hired, does not mean that these people have stopped thinking. They have just stopped thinking *for the organization*. They have become zombies, but only at work. The organization gets only what it wants of their minds, their other work gets the rest.

Sadly, most of these people have the impression that their bosses would be happy if they stayed where they are forever as long as they kept their heads down, which these people do. But these are intelligent, passionate people with a sense of mission. They won't lie low for long. As happened in my case, their accomplishments outside of the workplace fuel their spirit and their self-esteem. It is the organization, through mismanagement, that is losing. Like I was, these people are on the move. All vow to be somewhere else within the year.

Tips For Zombies

Do not wait as long as I did, *please*! Disengage your sense of accomplishment from what the boss thinks. He or she may be the greatest person, but not all people think alike. This person may never, ever, value you or your work. *Find a better match!* I was astounded at how appreciated and valued I was in other organizations. It is not about good guys and bad guys, it is about being in the right place with the right people. *Stand up, roll up your sleeping bag and move on!*

Ten Tips For Managers

When I do my participatory workshops on organizational change, I often ask people to relate the proverb that was most meaningful to them as they were growing up. It never ceases to amaze me how often people from North America and Europe quote the proverb, "Children should be seen and not heard." Contrast this with the African proverb: "It takes a whole village to raise one child." Our organizations are products of ourselves. They are extensions of the people who form them. They are like giant human beings, reflecting back, in giant form, who we are. We get back what we put in. As long as we are thinking, "Children should be seen and not heard," we build hierarchical organizations with competitiveness at their core, in which only certain people in the correct place in the hierarchy or with the correct titles are perceived as being worth listening to.

The tips for managers that emerged from the people I spoke with for this book all pointed to one central theme: co-operation. When these people started working in their organizations, there was a match between their mission and that of the organization. Their spirits were engaged and this constituted an unwritten agreement. When their spirits were dampened and became disengaged, the link was ruptured and the co-operation ended. The people's bodies continued working for the organization, but their spirits left.

I asked them: What do you need to keep your spirit engaged at work? What would have prevented you from taking your spirit elsewhere? Here are 10 tips they suggested:

1. Provide strong, committed, visionary leadership.
2. Ensure equality and respect for all.
3. Share information.
4. Value people.
5. Hire the right expertise.
6. Listen
7. Go for the gusto.
8. Have a vision. Make a match.
9. Give them the tools.
10. Get yourself out of the way.

1. Provide Strong, Committed, Visionary Leadership

People said that strong, committed visionary leadership is absolutely essential. It is the beginning of everything. Leaders with vision and the strength to remain committed and do whatever they must to further that vision, provide the beacon that enables people in their organizations to get through troubled waters. The people in organizations today can be compared to the sailors who signed on with Christopher Columbus. In these days of constant, unplanned change, today's organizational sailors may not have a map and they may not know what is around the next bend, but they do know that they want to work collectively to get to the New World, alive. People said repeatedly that they would hang in for the tough ride if they felt the leadership was strong, if they felt they could count on it when the going got rough.

People want the leaders of their organization to work together. When there is lack of co-ordination and explicit direction, chaos reigns and morale and productivity plummet. When there is not clear direction from the top, senior managers become competitive with one another for favor and particularly for resources. This gets transferred, indeed mimicked down the line and becomes the management culture of the organization.

I recently gave my third daughter, Alison, a copy of Canfield and Hansen's, *Chicken Soup for the Soul.* On page 85, she found the following poem by Dorothy L. Nolte.

Children Learn What They Live

If children live with criticism,
they learn to condemn.
If children live with hostility,
they learn to fight.
If children life with fear,
they learn to be apprehensive.

If children live with pity,
they learn to feel sorry for themselves.
If children live with ridicule,
they learn to be shy.
If children live with jealousy,
they learn what envy is.
If children live with shame,
they learn to feel guilty.
If children live with tolerance,
they learn to be patient.
If children live with encouragement,
they learn to be confident.
If children live with praise,
they learn to appreciate.
If children live with approval,
they learn to like themselves.
If children live with acceptance,
they learn to find love in the world.
If children live with recognition,
they learn to have a goal.
If children live with sharing,
they learn to be generous.
If children live with honesty and fairness,
they learn what truth and justice are.
If children live with security,
they learn to have faith in themselves and in those around them.
If children live with friendliness,
they learn that the world is a nice place in which to live.

If children live with sincerity,
they learn to have peace of mind
With what are your children living?

So it is in organizations. Senior managers set the tone of the organization by their vision, values and commitment to lead the ship through troubled waters. Their values and management style become reflected throughout the organization. If they encourage an unhealthy form of competitiveness, they get what they ask for. If they are inconsistent in their commitment to their vision, people waste countless amounts of energy vacillating, trying to figure out what they want. The goals become focused on pleasing management rather than enhancing the vision of the organization.

2. *Ensure Equality And Respect For All*

All of the people that I spoke with declared that they wanted to be treated with respect, as equals. The lack of respect and inequality manifested itself in two forms of bigotry—*hierarchical* and *stovepipe.*

What is *hierarchical bigotry*? I recently gave a keynote address at a conference for executive assistants, administrative assistants and secretaries. The stories they told could make one's hair stand on end. It is amazing how many people still treat secretaries as if they were servants. Secretaries are professionals, too. "Secretaries should be seen and not heard." That is hierarchical bigotry.

Other examples of hierarchical bigotry include: having your letter rerouted from the person you wrote, to someone down the line who is at the same level as you on the organizational chart; and not being allowed to speak to a vice-president about anything of consequence.

A company cannot operate without its support staff: secretaries, truck drivers and mail-room clerks. Respect is not inherent in any particular job. Do managers get more respect because they are more valuable or because they have power?

With so many of us becoming computer literate, the days of the secretary with the steno pad or dictaphone are gone. Enter the new secretary who can produce top-quality reports and presentation materials using the latest hardware and software technology. In organizations in which I have worked, secretaries of this calibre were rare and prized, yet administrative support staff, as a rule, are still treated as if they were second-class citizens. As in Israel and China, where bus drivers, I am told, can make as much money as medical doctors, we may soon see the day when the average secretary makes more money and is more respected than the middle manager.

Treating people as lesser beings, whether they are managers or secretaries, is an absolutely sure-fire way to disengage their spirit. Employees who feel valued and equal are happier and more productive. Creative teamwork and co-operative problem-solving are absolutely essential to keep spirit alive in the workplace.

Stovepipe bigotry exists when various units report to the top and exist virtually independently of one another, like stovepipes feeding into the main flue. Often, the members of these units do not work together or talk to one another unless absolutely necessary. What also happens in this situation is that units compete for work, favors and scarce resources. This is particularly true in situations where management has not clearly defined the roles of the units, creating duplication and overlap. Clients within and outside the organization become confused as to who provides which service. Clients then, naturally, shop around from unit to unit, thereby increasing competition among the stovepipes.

When there is clear direction from the top, supported by clear values and strong commitment, when the goals of each unit are linked with the essential vision, the beacon of the organization, stovepipes become a contradiction in terms. When people are all working together for the common good, they focus on keeping the boat afloat—not on throwing each other overboard—thus reaching the New World alive. If too many get thrown out, who will do the work to keep the ship sailing?

3. Share Information—Let It Flow Up And Down

To keep spirit alive in the workplace, people must be informed as quickly and as directly as possible on information affecting them and their work. This applies not only to circumstances concerning upcoming organizational changes or potential job losses, but also to information concerning the actual day-to-day work of the individual. People need to receive precise information and they also want to be able to pass important technical and professional information up the line. In the examples related in this book, information going in both directions seemed to get filtered numerous times. People wanted to be able to provide senior management with day-to-day contact with the field. This is particularly important for people in highly specialized, time-sensitive or politically sensitive positions.

Many people interviewed said that their work was negatively affected because they did not have a direct link to upper management. They required accurate information, but what information they were getting, more often than not, was watered down. People complained of getting more accurate information on corporate direction or new policies or programs from the newspapers or from clients than they did from the people above them in the organization.

As an example of what can happen when the lines of information are skewed, Russell, the biologist, spoke of a sustainable development task force that was set up with limited input from experts either on the line or in the field. Internal people had been trying to do this project for 10 years. Then a very expensive consultant was hired who did not take the time and trouble to get the input from the people who had been working on this for the preceding decade. This resulted, Russell said, in the recommendations of the task force making little sense and having no basis in reality. Not only did this dampen his spirit, it also upset him because it undermined a project that could have resulted in something far more positive for the environment.

4. Value People. Allow Mistakes

My second daughter, Stefanie, has an unsigned poster on her door. It shows a sad puppy and the following caption: "When I am good no one remembers. When I am bad, no one forgets."

To keep their spirit alive at work, people must feel that they make a difference. They want to go home at the end of the day thinking that their time on the job has some meaning. Managers and supervisors need to show people with words—and particularly with actions—that they value their employees and the work they do.

When people do a good job, they want to be recognized, acknowledged and even rewarded in some fashion. Money is not the issue here. Recognition is.

It was particularly important for people I interviewed that their managers or supervisors allow, indeed expect, them to make mistakes and to learn from them. They were tired of being blamed and made to feel guilty or inadequate. They kept repeating that people are not perfect machines, and systems are not perfect. Mistakes will happen. People wanted to hear their bosses say, "OK, where do we go from here?", rather than the all-too-common witch-hunt. They wanted managers to try harder to create a win-win rather than a win-lose situation. People wanted to see their bosses or supervisors supporting them rather than the project or case. They also wanted their bosses to know that the worker supported the project, too, and wanted to do their best. They wanted failures to be celebrated for what they had contributed to learning.

5. Hire The Expertise—Then Use It

People's spirit gets dampened when they see others being hired into management and supervisory positions for which they seem to have little or no expertise. The people I spoke with lamented that too often a person was put into a job because they were in line for something or because they were an ally of the manager, not necessarily because they were qualified. They could certainly understand the need for managers to have allies. They were aware of the value and importance of internal politics. However, when the person in question had very little expertise in a complex technical or professional area, the entire productivity of the unit was compromised and morale plummeted. People encouraged senior management to, "put the right person in the job, whatever it takes, please!"

The converse is also true. If you choose to hire an expert, do not put them in a corner and hire an "external" expert to do what the internal person used to do when they were external. People recounted numerous cases (it happened to me!) in which an employee with technical or professional expertise would be hired, usually from an external consulting firm or from an external private practice, only to be ignored. It was as if these people were perceived to have lost their intelligence the minute they signed that employment contract.

The people I interviewed recounted case after case of experts doing administrivia, while senior management spent thousands of dollars hiring external consultants with the same qualifications, and sometimes even their former colleagues. Money was wasted purchasing outside expertise that did not seem to be as good as those sitting doing nothing inside.

In addition, extra money had to be spent while these people "borrowed your watch to tell you the time." The external consultants had to take billable time to get to know the environment within the organization before they could begin the work. The internal consultant in the corner already knew the environment.

If you choose to hire internal expertise, use it. Part of the problem may be that managers expect external consultants to tell them what to do. When they pay them on contract, they expect them to know more. Managers do not seem to be as comfortable, however, seeking advice from their own employees. An unwritten rule comes into play, a rule that says the manager has to know more, that asking an employee for advice involves loss of "face."

It is important for managers to be receptive to, rather than frightened of, new information. The people I interviewed found that sometimes managers dismissed information before they fully understood it or its implications.

It is critical that managers be willing to learn from their employees and not expect to always have to be the ones who know the most about everything. People do not expect their managers to have all the answers. They expect them to have the *questions*. They want to see a willingness in management to learn from *them*. They want to be treated like the experts they are. They want to problem-solve together. They want to be asked for advice on what they were hired for. When they are not, they eventually turn off.

6. Listen

Managers must have good listening and questioning skills. Managers who could listen without judgment were perceived as rare. So were managers who could ask the right questions. All too often managers seemed to be so worried about having to provide answers that they did not listen long enough to get the full picture.

It is important for employees that managers and supervisors listen, particularly when something is going wrong. People find that often managers will shut down on hearing bad news and tell them to go fix it. They want their managers to listen longer. They do not want management to take over the job, they just want managers to guide them. Often this means helping people to ask themselves more and better questions.

When I do my seminars on surviving organizational transitions, I talk a lot about listening. I tell people that there are two important phrases to remember. The first is, "Listening is doing." People think that when someone comes to them with a problem, they must "do" something about it to get the person out of their misery. Usually, this is not the case. The person is in the process of solving the problem for themselves. Talking about it, or using someone for a sounding board, allows them to hear themselves think aloud and helps them to solve their problem. By listening without judgment—just listening—people help others with their problem more than if they were to offer a series of potential solutions. Most of the time, people with a problem will reject a series of offered solutions anyway. The listener is doing something to help by simply listening.

The second expression I ask people to remember is, "Whose monkey is this?" Who owns this problem? When we take over someone else's problem and solve it for them, we take away their power. By doing this, managers think that they are making things easier for an employee, for example, by taking away their aggravation. People are adults, not children. They have lots of experience dealing with aggravation in many different aspects of their lives. Working through a thorny problem provides opportunities to learn. When employees discuss problems or propose strange-sounding solutions, it is important to listen without judgment, help them ask themselves good questions, and let them continue problem-solving on their own.

7. Go For The Gusto—Take Responsibility

Managers must manage and leaders must lead. Whether your style is to lead the charge or support your people from behind, this responsibility cannot be shirked. This does not mean you have to know everything. It means that, if your employee goes out on a limb for you and someone starts to saw the limb off, it is not helpful to look the other way. Managers must not take on responsibilities that belong to their employees. This disempowers them. But managers must not create the monkeys either. Sometimes it is difficult to know where to draw the line. By and large, however, it works to go back to basics. If there is a corporate issue that is getting in the way of the job, it is the manager's job to help fix it. It is the manager's job to get the brambles out of the way so that the employee can have a clear path to do the work. The work is theirs. The corporate battles are yours. Many people spoke of programs being stalled for years while employees, who were hired to design and implement the programs, were politicking for permission. Countless letters were sent back and forth between lower-level employees who did not have the authority to make the decisions. If their bosses were to sit and have lunch with each other, take the bull by the horns and either get the permission to go ahead or stop the project, countless expensive hours could be saved.

People found that managers sometimes sloughed off difficult situations, indeed passing down to the employee problems that were not theirs to solve. Employees wanted managers to *do their job*. Employees, particularly during downsizings or mergers, were often asked to do things that were not their responsibility. In one case, a merger was happening between two large organizations. This was going to result in duplicate services in certain areas. If the two senior managers were involved in sorting this out, they hid it very well. The employees who reported to both senior managers had no idea of what the corporate structure was in the other organization and where they might fit in, yet they were being asked to choose if they wanted to come along or take advantage of outplacement packages. When employees asked for more information about the other organization, how they might fit in and what their work might be, they were told that the senior managers did not know and that they should call their counterpart at the other company and "work things out." The people involved in this merger were stressed enough. They wanted someone to steer the ship. Like these managers, Christopher Columbus was not sure of each step of the way, but he did not let go of the wheel.

8. Have A Vision. Make A Match

In order to keep people's spirits engaged, managers and supervisors have to have their spirits engaged also. People wanted to work for spirited leaders, for people who felt they had a mission, a vision for what they wanted to accomplish and how they were going to make a difference in the world.

People need to resonate not only with the vision of the organization, but also with the vision of their manager. There must be a match. Once, I accepted a position because I really resonated with the man performing the job interview. Unfortunately, he was outplaced a few days after I was hired. It took quite a while for his replacement to figure out quite what to do with me.

Once people's visions are matched with that of the organization and that of their boss, they need one more thing. People need to be encouraged to soar. It was not enough for the people I spoke with to have the same vision as their managers. They wanted their managers to encourage, indeed *expect* them to do things that were *extraordinary.* Like fledglings, they wanted to be pushed out of the nest to fly.

9. Give Them The Tools

How can a carpenter do the job without a hammer? Once the mission of the employee and the organization are matched, it is critical that employees be given the tools they need to do the job. There are four different kinds of tools.

First, people need material resources including things such as an appropriate budget, equipment, reference materials and information. Second, they need appropriately trained and available human resources. They need staff! Third, they need an adequate level of decision-making latitude. They have to be allowed to do their job in a way that is acceptable to themselves. They must be allowed to make or at least influence decisions affecting their work.

The last critical tool in getting the job done without dampening spirit is realistic deadlines. This was perceived as particularly important by people in highly technical fields who were supervised by managers who did not have the same level of knowledge. When managers combined lack of expertise with not listening and not allowing information up the line, what often resulted were expensive, signed contracts with deadlines that were technically impossible to meet.

10. Get Yourself Out Of The Way

It is very important for managers to have a sense of balance and peace within themselves. People found that insecurity exhibited by their managers was a demon that kept rearing its ugly head. This problem often came up when people had an area of expertise that was different from their managers. Their managers seemed to have difficulty letting them do their thing—as if they were concerned that they would not be able to control their employees. Like my boss in the story recounted earlier, these people's managers could not seem to find a way to manage them without dampening their spirit.

We cannot all know everything. When managing someone with a certain level of expertise, it is important to find ways that enable you to trust the person. You may not be able to trust the information, but perhaps you can find a way to ensure that it is all right to trust the person. If it turns out that they were correct, everyone wins.

Another situation that often put managers off balance occurred when there was an agency or body to please. Approval of funding agencies or of the public were particularly strong motivators. In these cases, the prime objective became what people would think rather than the truth. Only acceptable truth was OK, even if it was not true.

I hope the days of telling agencies and people what they want to hear rather than the truth will soon be in the past. Not telling the truth not only dampens people's spirit, it wastes time and money and can be dangerous. These days, everything is moving too quickly for us to waste time with lies. Stopping corporate lying begins with each one of us. Daily, we are faced with difficult situations and must make decisions whether or not to take the moral path and tell the truth. The new way starts with each of us, today.

TEN TIPS SUMMARY

Ten things that managers can do to keep spirit alive, vibrant and engaged at work.

1. ***Provide Strong, Committed, Visionary Leadership.***
   Be like Christopher Columbus—a beacon in troubled waters.
2. ***Ensure Equality And Respect For All.***
   Eliminate hierarchical and stovepipe bigotry.
3. ***Share Information. Let It Flow Up And Down.***
   Employees need it to get their work done. And so do you.
4. ***Value People. Allow Mistakes.***
   Support the people as well as the project.
5. ***Hire The Expertise—then Use It.***
   Put the right person in the job, whatever it takes.
6. ***Listen.***
   "Listening is doing." Listen without judgment.
   "Whose monkey is this?" Doing too much for people disempowers them.
7. ***Go For The Gusto.***
   Take responsibility—do what is yours to do.
8. ***Have A Vision. Make A Match.***
   Be a visionary. Hire people who share your dream.
9. ***Give Them The Tools.***
   People need four things: material resources, staff, appropriate authority and realistic time frames.
10. ***Get Yourself Out Of The Way.***
    Don't let insecurity or fear spoil a good idea. Tell the truth. Lies sabotage.

Why Haven't We Got It Yet?

Not too long ago, while I was visiting a company to give a talk, it happened to be "casual dress day." I saw an employee wearing a T-shirt which had the following phrase printed on the front: "I ran out of sick leave so I called in dead!"

If we have known for 50 years that people and passion are the keys to corporate success, why have we not achieved it yet? Why are we still making the same spirit-dampening corporate blunders a half century later? So many levels of employees seem to blame those above them. This goes all the way to the top and then, not surprisingly, back down the ladder again. Managers and supervisors blame the people below. Ridiculous! Speak to the very leader whom 50 people are crying into their soup about and surprisingly, you will often find a committed, hard-working person who is swimming as fast as possible, reading management books, attending seminars with peers, even going for professional counselling on how to cope. The same is often true of the employees below them. What is going on?

Pace Of Change

With the global economy, the rapid pace of change, technological developments and multiple downsizings and restructurings, the ground is shifting so rapidly that many of us do not know how to begin to keep up. We speak of the new employee contract, that organizations cannot give the same guarantees that they did in the past. Before, if one worked hard and was loyal, one could be guaranteed a job with the company for as long as it was in business. Now, we are told, our only security rests within ourselves—in developing our skills and keeping them sharp. But we are not computers. How do we do it?

Computers can be reprogrammed to do new, different and wonderful things. Microchips can be added and memory can be expanded. Humans, however, are not like Commander Data, the android from the starship Enterprise on the television series *Star Trek: The Next Generation.* We cannot have parts removed and replaced. We cannot be upgraded in the same way as computers can.

A Wiser Workforce

The Greying Boomers

People often choose a different pace as they get older. Brains get crowded with information people have acquired throughout their lives and memory for trivia becomes less acute. People often become wiser, more peaceful and more spiritual. What may have been a mind-only model expands to a more holistic approach to life and work. People begin to look for opportunities to contribute in broader ways.

Our population is greying. This is adding new dimensions to our workforce. When the baby boomers had small children, we saw the advent of child-proof caps on medicine bottles. Now many boomers have eyesight that cannot read the small print that tells how to open the bottle and fingers with the beginnings of arthritis that cannot get the pain medicine bottle open. People will not buy products they cannot read or get open. On drug store shelves, we now see pain medications with large grippable caps and big-print instructions. Just as we see new packaging in drug stores, so do we see different reading material in book stores.

Youthful Wisdom

In 1982, when I began working with clients on the connection between stress and illness, even my own parents treated me as if I were selling snake oil. This is not the case today. The holistic perspective, that is, the concept that there is a connection between mind, body, heart and soul is pervasive. Even my teenager can predict, from looking at their level of stress, when the other members of our family are going to become sick. She is not the only one who is becoming wise at a younger age. We are starting to see more heart and soul in workplaces today. I notice this when I give my talks to large audiences. When other speakers pitch only to people's heads, audience members turn off and walk out. They have been reading books that speak to their souls. Look at some of the recent best-sellers. To name only a few, there are Thomas Moore's *Care of the*

Soul and *Soulmates*; James Redfield's *Celestine Prophecy*; John Grey's *Men are from Mars, Women are from Venus* and *What Your Mother Didn't Tell You and your Father Didn't Know*; and Steven Covey's *Seven Habits of Highly Effective People*. All of these books speak to people on a variety of levels and involve much more than their minds.

When speakers address people's minds, hearts and souls, people listen intently and are very moved by the presentation. This is what they want. People in their 20s and 30s are bringing to the workplace a much broader perspective than was acceptable even 10 years ago. People are becoming wiser at a younger age. This cannot help but make workplaces different.

Management Musings and Canine Counsel

The Passion Or The Paycheck?

Those of us who choose to work for organizations, particularly in the public sector, are sometimes motivated more by service than by money. When we join organizations, we indenture ourselves. We join, not as partners, but more as people enlist in the military. We know people above us will be calling the shots and we sign on because we share a mission and think we have a better chance of completing it together.

Now, we are told to become entrepreneurs within organizations. For most of us, this involves developing a whole new set of skills that we probably do not have and may not be interested in acquiring. In addition, career bureaucrats have no idea how to manage entrepreneurs.

So what do we get? We get employees at two extremes. Some employees are spiritual Rip van Winkles. Their souls fell asleep on the job years ago. Their spirit is fulfilled outside of the office and they give of their souls only what the office can handle, which is often very little. Managers often waste considerable time either trying to keep these people down or wake them up. At the other end of the continuum, we have people who are like Jonathan Livingston Seagull in the book by Richard Bach. They are soaring, taking off to new heights. Often these people are managed by a perplexed group of managers who are not quite sure what to do with them.

Managers are faced with a double-edged sword. Their people are all over the map: from those who have a strong sense of mission to those who are just putting in time and do not seem to care. How have we managed so far in this new era?

More Of The Same

At a management meeting not too long ago, I participated in a group discussion led by a consultant who was trying to get us to find a metaphor for our team. We were a group of directors of personnel from branch offices across the country plus a few specialists like myself. Some said we were like an orchestra, all playing different instruments, yet harmonizing to the same music. Some said we were like the Starship Enterprise—a team working together to soar to new heights and explore new worlds. In the end, we learned that we could not find one single metaphor to describe ourselves. The exercise was a disaster, or was it? Were we unsuccessful because we were a competitive, non-trusting, non-compliant group of poor communicators? Or was this a sign of the times? What is a metaphor for organizations of today?

On library shelves today, there are countless management books in a variety of styles to appeal to a variety of readerships, learning styles, management styles and personalities. Among the pages are many wonderful theories, which were great successes when they were written and remain classics because they fill a need. Perhaps, however, something is still missing.

What do virtually all management theories that have been written so far have in common? Management, of course. Some authors call it leadership and there are clear theories differentiating one concept from the other. A manager plans, organizes, directs and keeps the ship afloat. A manager makes sure the machinery runs well and people are doing their jobs and the unit is doing what it is supposed to do, and doing it well. A leader is a visionary who sets the tone of an organization, takes it into the future and encourages the company and its employees to outshine the competition. But what do the two have in common? What leadership and management theory have in common is that the senior manager or leader is top dog, the leader of the pack.

Speaking Of Dogs

I used to think that everything I knew about management I learned from my kids. But my Labrador pup, Gilligan Sparky, in the four months he was with us, taught me more. At the Centre for Applied Canine Behaviour, they taught me that dogs are pack animals and

Gilligan had first to learn that he was not the leader. We had to teach him who the leader was and what Gilligan's ordinal position was in the household. We had to teach him our culture: when we ate, when we slept, who walked him and his relationship to the other animals. How is this different from what happens to a new employee in an organization?

When we start in an organization, we have an independent spirit, just like Gilligan. We join that organization rather than another because we see a fit. However, we then have to fit our spirit into the culture of that organization. We come full face against a culture or philosophy that ranks management, in varying levels, up to the top of a ladder. We hear of flat organizations—those with very few organizational levels—but no matter how flat an organization is, there is always someone at the top; someone who owns the company or is the president or chairs the board of directors.

I know two psychologists who started a consulting firm together. As the company got bigger, they had to hire administrative support staff and junior associates, who ended up on salary or percentage or both, but not as equal partners. There is still someone—in this case—the partners, at the top. One of the partners lamented, "I can't believe it, I'm turning into a bureaucracy! I hate it. This is exactly what I left organizations to avoid."

What We Expect Of People At The Top

In organizations, do we have clear definitions of what being at the top means? I was fortunate enough to receive teacher-training in the experimental 1970s. This was when we threw the textbooks into the wastebasket and taught by objectives and themes. The most fundamental thing I learned in teacher-training is something that has changed my working life forever. It affected how I taught, how I raised my children and how I dealt with the people who worked for me. I learned that there would always be children in my class, even at age 10, who were smarter than I was and knew more than I did.

I learned that it was my duty to ensure that they not only knew more than I did, but also had the capacity to learn more than I knew and be better than I was at many things. Because, even back then, the pace of change was more rapid than we had ever seen. We were already into the information age. I learned that even if I succeeded in teaching the children all I knew, this would not prepare them for the world they were about to enter. I learned that my objective was to give them the tools they needed in order to learn and to get myself out of their way. Although this philosophy is not as easy to put in place as it sounds, I believe it has relevance in management today.

Change That Paradigm: Tame Those Monsters

Teachers and managers have much in common. With the job comes a feeling of obligation. By definition, we feel that we have to know more and be able to advise the people below us on issues, decisions, etc. If people come to us with a problem and we do not have an answer, we often feel inadequate, as if we are not doing our job properly. Imagine how I felt as a Grade 7 music teacher when I realized that Johnny could play the piano much better than I could.

Since my piano is lousy and this was a real sore point, Johnny definitely hit a sensitive key for me.

Like teachers, managers can feel that they are failures, that they are not doing their jobs properly and that one day, someone will find out and they could lose their jobs. They can feel that the Johnnys of the organization make them look inadequate.

What do you do if you feel your future, your life is at stake? You protect yourself, of course. Many teachers, fearing they will not "look good" never let Johnny near the piano. Johnny at work gets put in a similar corner and is kept off projects. Johnny is prevented from shining for two reasons. First, the manager is insecure and afraid of looking bad or inadequate or, worst of all, stupid, and second, the manager does not know how to manage a person of Johnny's calibre. The manager is afraid that Johnny will get out of control. According to Captain Jean-Luc Picard of the Starship Enterprise in the television series *Star Trek: The Next Generation*, "Most acts of aggression are committed not out of malice, but out of an instinct for self preservation."

So What Do We Do Now?

Two things have to happen for things to change. First, we have to change dramatically the way we look at management and leadership. We are asking our employees to soar into the next century, but we do not know how to get them to soar or to manage them once they do. The first is like trying to waken the dead. The second is like trying to control fireworks.

To waken the dead, we have to remember that it is the organization and we, their managers as agents of that organization, who put them to sleep in the first place. Indeed, we encouraged this to happen. We managed them as if we were on a farm or in a factory. We treated them like chickens in a coop. We bought the healthiest chickens we could find, placed them in a coop, fed them well and told them to lay eggs. If one chicken decided it wanted to become an eagle and soar through the roof, what happened? Bang! "We're having chicken tonight!"

The same thing happened with workhorses. They were supposed to pull ploughs. If one decided to become a racehorse, he got sold or turned into glue. Why? Because the farmer had not succeeded in "breaking his spirit." We have deliberately broken people's spirits to make them fit into our work culture. The question that we are still struggling to answer is: how do we get loyal, dependable employees without breaking them?

Lessons From My Dog

Gilligan was absolutely unmanageable. He jumped up on people with his jaws open, scaring them half to death. He pulled on the leash to the extent that I thought of entering him in a truck-pulling contest. To adopt this dog into our already crowded family was an exercise in sheer, unbridled insanity. What could have possessed me? Was I losing my mind? Was I not busy enough with a very responsible full-time job and writing this book on the side? How many hours did I think there were in a day? And, as my mother said when she heard about Gilligan's adoption, "Don't you have enough expenses?"

During a very difficult period in my life, I got a lot of solace from Ann Morrow Lindbergh's book *Gift from the Sea*. She spoke of the life's lessons she learned by observing sea shells. I did not grow up by the sea. I was raised in a province of rivers. A walk by the river is never the same two days in a row. The light changes, the shadows change. One never knows what the view will be around the next bend even if one walks that path every day. I now live two minutes from a beautiful walking path by the edge of a river. Before the arrival of Gilligan, I had been living here for six months and gone walking there only a few times. Gilligan gave me no choice. Every morning at sunrise and evening at sunset, we went walking by the river. Not only did I get exercise and peace (when I was not having my arm tugged off), but as I observed Gilligan's behavior, his socialization, and how his training was or was not progressing, I learned things about managing spirit. It was a humbling experience.

The Police-Dog Academy or Behavior Therapy

This was nuts! Gilligan and I had to go to school. Choke chain or lure / reward, that was the question. I started with the "police-dog academy," the tough choke-chain approach. My dog was tough, none of that weak stuff for my Gilligan. After all, he was part German Shepherd, I think. After one lesson, the dog was starting to heel, but he also had a very bad cough and cowered at the sight of the instructor. Although we are not sure, the vet said the cough may have been caused by the choke chain. Our other dog never got the cough so it was probably caused by an injury, not an infection. When we did some homework and heard that others had had similar experiences with this type of training, we decided to go for the "nice" academy—behavior therapy. Training this way takes longer. Five weeks into the training, Gilligan was still nuts, but he sat quietly, did not cower from the instructor and the cough disappeared with the choke chain. He learned to listen, slowly. He was learning our culture, what was all right and what was not, and his eyes still sparkled. He might have heeled faster in the other class, but I was willing to pay the price for a dog whose spirit was not broken.

Management or supervision with power and intimidation is something we all know well. If people are afraid of us, of the power we have over their careers, they will do somersaults. They will cowtow. They will also sit in a corner and do nothing if that is what it takes to get a good appraisal. Unfortunately, that is what many of the people in this study did. Hard-line managers, those who managed like the "police-dog academy," wanted to create employees in their image. Different, creative people, who turned problems on their ear and attacked them sideways, from new angles, sometimes at considerable savings to the organization, were not welcome. They were "strange." They were criticized for not being good managers if they did not manage in the authoritarian, autocratic style of their managers. They had to be "broken."

It worked. Congratulations, you lose! These people got their spirits broken—but only at work. Those who were managed in this way were the most passive-aggressive and the most damaging to their organizations of all the employees in the study. They not only became determined to keep their spirits alive *despite* the manager, but they often did it on company time and used company resources. They did what a former Jesuit priest tells me is called "Occult Compensation." They did little things such as taking books and supplies, and copying computer programs for use on their home computers. They developed an I'll-show-you attitude that fuelled them in their outside pursuits.

Jumping In

Since Gilligan was a black Labrador retriever, with jowls and webbed toes, he was a water dog. It was fascinating to watch him discover the river. On our first walk by the river in mid-April, the water was still quite cold and partially frozen. We were accompanied by my friend JoAnn and her seasoned Labrador, Lily. Lily exuberantly raced into the water chasing this most fascinating toy. Gilligan, like many new employees, dove right in. He nearly drowned himself, never mind froze to death. Gilligan came smack up against the "corporate culture" of the water.

Passionate employees are particularly vulnerable to jumping in too soon. A communications expert for a large government department did just that. He was so excited about the potential contribution he could make to a department undergoing a major transition that he threw himself into a major project immediately. He did excellently on the project, but unfortunately, he told the senior manager the truth, something that he did not know she was unable to hear. Just like Gilligan, he got in over his head. People make mistakes. Unfortunately, this person's manager was not as forgiving as the river. His career never recovered. What saved his soul was that the organization came up with an early retirement scheme. He was backed into a smaller and smaller corner until he had no option but to leave. Pity!

Chaos

One warm July evening, I was sitting on a large rock by the water while Gilligan explored the shallows. The river was as calm as a mirror. Then a motor boat went by. All of a sudden, Gilligan's water changed. It became choppy and chaotic with waves from the boat. Gilligan suddenly became very alert. His ears perked up, his eyes sparkled and his muscles tensed. Off he darted, still in the shallows, trying to bite the waves. Something had gone "wrong" with his water. His first impulse, when the water got choppy, was to try to stop it. He raced back and forth along the shore, nipping at the waves, determined to get this water under control. He did not stop until he succeeded.

This is our first impulse in organizations also. The minute the water gets rough, we try to calm it down. We cannot tolerate chaos. We forget that chaos precedes change. We make the mistake of biting the waves, of preventing the chaos from happening because we are afraid. Spirit in the workplace often appears like choppy water. The calmness comes alive. It ripples with life and we do not know exactly what storm may be ahead. We become afraid and try to stop the waves. Change, like waves, cannot be stopped. Neither can spirit. When we try to keep the waters calm all the time, we stunt the growth of our employees *and* our organization.

Challenge

On one of our earlier walks, Gilligan came upon a very large branch. Retriever that he was, he decided that this branch definitely had to be brought home. Unfortunately, the branch was significantly larger than he was. In addition, Gilligan had not yet learned his physics lesson on leverage. He did not know yet that it is best to carry a branch from the middle. I watched with amusement as he struggled, alternately tripping himself and getting the branch tangled up in his leash. He was determined and he dragged that branch as if his life depended on it. I finally took pity on him, broke the branch in two and gave to him what I thought was a manageable chunk. Mistake! He carried it for about two seconds then lost interest.

Like Gilligan, employees get bored when the job is too easy and has no challenge. People need to be encouraged to stretch themselves, not only to be creative, but also to find solutions to problems on their own. That is not to say that managers should abdicate their responsibilities. It is important to determine an appropriate amount of decision-making responsibility. Too little can be just as harmful as too much.

Manager As Puppeteer

Many years ago, I spent some time as a professional puppeteer touring nursery and elementary schools in both San Francisco and Toronto. As I think back on those years, I discover a metaphor for management that I use in my talks about this book.

Marionettes! We all remember them from, it seems, a long time ago. But from the perspective of a puppeteer, how are marionettes operated? Someone *above* them is manipulating them, pulling their strings.

But the puppets we used in our shows were called hand-and-rod puppets. With these puppets, one of the puppeteer's hands operates the mouth and the other manipulates a rod attached to another part of the puppet. These puppets are operated from *below,* with the puppeteer's hands held high in the air.

As a metaphor for management, marionettes are limited by someone pulling the strings above them. Hand-and-rod puppets, however, put puppeteering on the map and are used in very successful television shows such as *Sesame Street*. When supported from below, people, like those puppets, can reach for new heights.

The Farm Or The Olympics

Workhorses or racehorses? Chickens or eagles? The choice is ours. I fear, however, that those companies that continue to prefer workhorses and chickens or, as in the example above, marionettes, will cease to exist. If we limit the performance or soaring of our people by the fact that they cannot soar higher than their manager or than senior management of the organization, then we are limited by the potentially narrow vision of one person, or the capacities of one manager. Spirited employees who are perceived as unmanageable are limited by the manager's perceived inability to control.

We have to do our homework on ourselves. No one is perfect. We often hold ourselves back with insecurities and limiting beliefs. One of our most limiting beliefs is perhaps not so much the fear of failure as the fear of success. We are caterpillars who have been going in and out of the cocoon for decades, never quite ready to finish the job and become butterflies. What are we afraid of? Perhaps we are afraid of ourselves, of our own power.

I have worked in counselling with many people experiencing mid-life crisis. I have helped people go through downsizings in which they had to tear apart the very organization they spent 20 years building. I have also put in place programs for people who had been traumatized by a critical incident on the job such as being held up at gunpoint or the death of a colleague.

Mid-life crises, downsizings and critical incidents on the job were often life changing events. A psychological wall inside crumbled and these people started to feel. Often they thought that they were losing it and did not think they could survive emotionally. They had never had such powerful feelings before. Research has taught us, however, that allowing these feelings and acknowledging that they are normal is the first step in healing. When a bad cut is healing, it swells and forms a scab. It looks worse before it gets better. Psychological healing often occurs the same way.

We block ourselves. We avoid that ugly swelling and scab forming emotional stage. We have taught ourselves that expressing emotion in the workplace is not all right. Only our minds are welcome. It seems as if all emotions, even the positive ones, have been perceived as negative. Our spirits cannot soar if we are shut down emotionally. We cannot turn into butterflies if we are afraid to go into the cocoon and stay there, enduring the chaos, uncertainty and sometimes even pain, until we evolve.

Where do we begin? We begin by acknowledging the normalcy of feelings in the workplace, particularly the positive ones such as passion and enthusiasm. The word enthusiasm is from the Greek words, en Theos—in God. When we are enthusiastic, it means our spirit is engaged. We are in touch with that spark of the divine within us. Once we get used to our feelings, we learn that they are not all bad, and they cease to scare us. Then we can deal with our own personal monsters, our own limiting beliefs about ourselves, the beliefs that make us afraid to let each other soar.

Once we face and begin to tame our own monsters, then we will all be free. We will be able to soar ourselves and it will not scare us half to death when others soar. We will know that they will not go crashing out of control through the roof. When organizations allow the spirit of their employees to soar, the only thing that goes crashing through the roof is the bottom line.

References

Bach, R. (1973). *Jonathan Livingston Seagull.* New York: Avon.

Canfield, J. and Hansen, M.V. (1993). *Chicken Soup for the Soul.* Florida: Health Communications.

Covey, S. (1989). *The Seven Habits of Highly Effective People.* New York: Simon and Schuster.

Gray, J. (1992). *Men are from Mars, Women are from Venus.* New York: Harper Collins.

Gray, J. (1994). *What Your Mother Didn't Tell You and Your Father Didn't Know.* New York: Harper Collins.

Harvey, J.B. (1988). *The Abilene Paradox and other Meditations on Management.* Lexington MA: Lexington Books.

The Kingston Trio. *MTA* on *The Best of the Kingston Trio.* USA: Capitol Records

Lindbergh, A.M. (1965). *Gift from the Sea.* New York: Vintage Books

Moore, T. (1992). *Care of the Soul.* New York: Harper Collins.

Moore, T. (1994). *Soulmates.* New York: Harper Collins.

Peters, T.J. and Waterman, R.H. (1982). *In Search of Excellence.* New York: Harper and Row.

Rand, A. (1957) *Atlas Shrugged.* New York: Random House.

Redfield, J. (1993). *Celestine Prophecy.* New York: Warner

SURVIVING ORGANIZATIONAL INSANITY

KEEPING *Spirit Alive* AT WORK

by Sharon Rolbin, Ph.D.

Please send me ______ copies of *Surviving Organizational Insanity.*

I have enclosed a check payable to: Lightkeeper

_____ x $15.95 Cdn + $3.00 (shipping & handling) = __________

_____ x $12.95 US + $3.00 (shipping & handling) = __________

Name ______________________________

Address ______________________________

City ______________________________

Province / State ______________________________

Postal Code / (Zip) ______________________________

Telephone: (   ) __________ Fax: (   ) __________

Send orders to:

Lightkeeper
2445 Ogilvie Road,
Gloucester, Ontario, Canada K1J 7N3
Tel (613) 747-6933
Fax (~~416~~ 613) 747-8440

Special discounts on large orders:

25 copies or more – 10%
100 copies or more – 20%
500 copies or more – 30%

❑ Please send me information on Dr. Rolbin's seminars and keynotes

SURVIVING *ORGANIZATIONAL* INSANITY

KEEPING *Spirit Alive* AT WORK

by Sharon Rolbin, Ph.D.

Please send me ______ copies of *Surviving Organizational Insanity.*

I have enclosed a check payable to: Lightkeeper

_____ x $15.95 Cdn + $3.00 (shipping & handling) = __________

_____ x $12.95 US + $3.00 (shipping & handling) = __________

Name ______________________________

Address ______________________________

City ______________________________

Province / State ______________________________

Postal Code / (Zip) ______________________________

Telephone: (   ) ______________ Fax: (   ) ______________

Send orders to:

Lightkeeper
2445 Ogilvie Road,
Gloucester, Ontario, Canada K1J 7N3
Tel (613) 747-6933
Fax ~~(416)~~ 613 747-8440

Special discounts on large orders:

25 copies or more – 10%
100 copies or more – 20%
500 copies or more – 30%

❑ Please send me information on Dr. Rolbin's seminars and keynotes